GATEW

Tony Castle

GATEWAY
TO THE TRINITY

Meditations on Rublev's Icon

 St Paul Publications

St Paul Publications
Middlegreen, Slough SL3 6BT, England

Copyright © St Paul Publications 1988

Cover artwork by Mary Lou Winters

Typeset by the Society of St Paul, Ireland

Printed by Billing and Sons, Worcester

ISBN 085439 273 4

St Paul Publications is an activity of the priests and brothers of the Society of St Paul who proclaim the Gospel through the media of social communication

Contents

Dedicated to
Sister Maria and Sister Noreen
and all the Sisters
of the Daughters of St Paul

Introduction

The 'Hospitality of Abraham' first came to my attention when I was browsing around the bookshop at Nashdom Abbey, some fifteen years ago. I have to confess that I bought the Icon knowing nothing about it and for the wrong reasons! My wife and I were just setting up home and icons, we knew, were becoming the fashionable things to have! It hung, largely ignored, on the walls of our home for the next ten years, in the company of other pictures. The big change came after I had read a little about the Icon and one of the ever-kind Daughters of St Paul, at their London Book Centre, gave me a poster representing the Icon. Not long afterwards I used the poster as a visual aid while speaking about the Holy Trinity and I soon recognised its value as a stimulant to meditation. From then on the Icon began to 'speak' to me (see the body of the text for an explanation of icon language).

This book has not been written in the quiet of a monastery or convent, but with great difficulty against the background of a noisy family of four children (plus friends) under twelve years of age. Thomas, who is two, has offered to help me on numerous occasions and cannot be side-tracked until he has had 'a go' on the typewriter! In spite of the inevitable family interruptions I am convinced that the family is the proper setting for thoughts on the Holy Trinity, as I hope the book will show.

I would like to acknowledge that several of the illustrative stories originate from a priest friend, who does not wish to be named. I would also like to express my gratitude to Mrs Jacquie Galley who typed the final copy of the manuscript.

Tony Castle

Chapter One

The Incarnation, Key to Icons

We have just received through the door of our home a National Shoppers' Survey offering us £10's worth of money-off coupons if we complete and return the Shopping Survey. It really is very comprehensive with fifty-seven questions, all of which are subdivided, ranging from the type and brands of coffee we buy to the languages we speak; not omitting to ask about our favourite T.V. programmes and the ages of any dogs we might have and their body weight! All this, of course, is to be fed into a computer somewhere so that, I quote, 'you don't miss out on free coupons and sample mailings!'

It was section 49, 'Leisure Interests' that really caught my eye and preserved the survey from the bin. Book reading, camping etc., is followed predictably by golf, model making and 36 other leisure pursuits. Included at no. 29 is *Religious Activities*! Well there you have it! If anyone ever doubted what the general secular world thinks of religion, it should now be clear. It is a leisure pursuit. The movement towards secularisation that began in the 17th century, was given a name in Victorian times and intensified in the last hundred years, is now complete. Christianity with its Good News of Salvation is considered to be nothing more than a leisure activity on a par

11

with golf and stamp-collecting! The teaching of the Incarnation ('the Word was made flesh and dwelt among us') which places the sacred at the very heart of the secular is rendered impotent. As an aside it is interesting to note that the very commercial interests that have produced and promoted the National Shopping Survey are the same that will whip up the public to a spending spree and a fever of excitement about Christmas.

For the Christian the Incarnation is at the centre of his Faith just as his religion is at the centre of his life, giving it meaning and purpose. The Incarnation is not some historical event of nearly 2,000 years ago but a living, daily reality placing the sacred at the very heart of the secular, as the spirit is in the body. The material things of life, for those with the eyes of Faith, point the way to the spiritual. 'By virtue of the Incarnation, nothing here below is profane for those who know how to see' (Teilhard de Chardin, *Le Milieu Divin*). St Thomas Aquinas said 'Grace builds on nature', which can be understood to mean that the visible material things about us can lead us to an understanding of the invisible, the Divine. If the ordinary ingredients of life like water, oil, bread and wine, that are used in the Sacraments, can open up a way for us to the world of the Spirit, cannot images painted on wood, or plaster, laid out in mosaic or enamelled on metal do the same? That is the belief of Eastern Orthodox Christians. The role of Icons and the reverence accorded them can only be understood and appreciated if there is some understanding of the essential meaning of the Incarnation.

The word 'icon' comes from the Greek word for 'image' (*eikwv*) and can be applied, as it was in the beginning, to a statue, a picture made of mosaic or a drawing scratched on the walls of a catacomb. Over the centuries, the word has become more strictly associated with representations painted upon wood, plaster etc., which represent an historical event from Scripture, or a saintly person.

The reader may notice that here and throughout the book, I scrupulously avoid equating the word icon with 'picture', this is because what the Western mind and eye understands by 'picture' and what the Orthodox Christian understands by 'icon' are totally different. When the icon-painter settles down to work he or she is bound to follow quite strict rules (see pages 14-15, 17-18) and with his skill and paints he intends to open a window for us on to the Divine.

The Orthodox Church teaches that God is revealed to us not only by words (which the Western Church has emphasised) but also by images; in other words, God's revelation is not just to the human ear but to the eye as well. The Eastern Church asks us to consider that Christ is not just the Word of God (Jn 1:1) but also the Image of God. 'He is the image of the unseen God' (Col 1:15; Jn 1:18 and Heb 1:3). A consideration of this reveals why the great Christian theologians, like St Basil and St John Chrysostom gave unreserved support to the use and veneration of icons. And St Theodore of Studios (759-826) could say of icons, 'whatever is marked there with paper and ink (the Scriptures), the same is marked on

13

the icon with various pigments or some other material'.

While the Mosaic Law strictly forbade the use of images of the unseen God in Judaism, Christians, from the beginning, appreciated that God was made visible to them in and through Christ. To have seen Christ was to have seen the Father (the very words of Jesus to Philip, Jn 14:9); so to have an image of Christ was acceptable and, even more than that, desirable as a means of revealing God to us.

In his book, *The Meaning of Icons,* Leonid Ouspensky reminds us that the art of painting portraits was very popular in the Roman Empire at the time of Christ. A firm tradition exists in the Orthodox Church that an image of the Saviour did date from his own lifetime; and not long afterwards of Mary also. The Church historian, Eusebius, writing about 330 AD, says,

> 'I have seen a great many portraits of the Saviour, of Peter and of Paul, which have been preserved up to our own time.'
> (*History of the Church,* Book VII, Ch.18)

When the Bishops gathered for the seventh Ecumenical Council in order to discuss the theology of icons and draw up rules and regulations governing them they confirmed the early use of images in the Christian Church. They said, 'the tradition of making images existed even at the time of the preaching of Christianity by the Apostles.' Certainly, by the time of the fourth century the great Christian writers and theologians, like St Basil the Great and St John

14

Chrysostom take the veneration of icons for granted as a well established tradition of Church life and practice.

> 'The silent painting speaks on the walls and does much good.'
>
> (St Gregory of Nyssa)

Throughout the period we have just been referring to the Christians of Rome were painting on the walls of the catacombs symbolic and pictorial expressions of their Faith. For example, what would a youth surrounded by sheep mean to a Roman pagan or a bread basket with a fish lying across the top?

The first official Church statement on Icons was at the Synod of Trullan (692 AD) and nearly a hundred years later, at the Second Council of Nicaea (787) strict guidelines were laid down. These were in keeping with the suggestions made in Pope Hadrian I's letter to the Council. The veneration of icons was upheld as long as they were given a relative love, absolute adoration was to be reserved to God alone, so that the honour given to the image was to pass on to that which was represented.

So the image was considered to be a doorway to the Divine or a window opening on to the sacred. The icon received its dignity by sharing a degree of the reverence due to the sacred original. The Council's teaching acknowledged how gradually the understanding had grown that the material world was able to transmit a revelation of the Divine world, making it more accessible to human understanding and contemplation. The

Council Fathers placed icons on exactly the same level of dignity as the scriptures and the cross, as one of the forms of revelation and knowledge of God. While the decisions of the Second Council of Nicaea were as acceptable to the Western Church as to the Eastern, it was in fact the Orthodox Churches who retained and developed the liturgical use of images while the Latin Church placed more emphasis upon the cross of Christ.

There is a story of a modern parish priest who was building a new church. From an Orthodox monastery in England he commissioned an icon for the Lady chapel. Suddenly, the official opening day of the church seemed to be upon him and he had not received the icon. Rather concerned he rang the monastery and spoke to the abbot. 'I've been expecting delivery of the icon,' the parish priest said. 'It is finished,' said the monk, 'and we have been expecting you to call and collect it.' 'I've been much too busy to get down to you,' replied the parish priest, 'could you please pop it in the post to us.' There was a silence from the other end, then the abbot said, 'An icon is a sacred object and we would never just put it in the post.' The parish priest was lost for words, there was a pause, then the abbot added, 'I suppose I could send Sister Thecla'. The priest was relieved to hear this suggestion and generously responded with, 'Sister must stay for lunch'. There was another short patient silence, and the Orthodox monk replied, 'Thank you, Father, but Sister Thecla will be fasting while she is carrying the icon to you and returning!'

The morning arrived and the parish priest himself opened the door to Sister Thecla, who without a word, bowed her head, presented the parcel and in silence, withdrew.

With a knowledge of this background to icons one can understand why in devout Orthodox homes, the icons arranged in a special corner or area are incensed morning and evening. A large proportion of icons are of Mary, the Mother of God, and it is very noticeable that in contrast with the statues and images of the Western Church she is never represented alone. Very often the Child, who always accompanies her, is depicted with an adult face and, by a gesture or an inclination of the Mother's head or eyes, it is quite clear that the Child is being presented to us. That, of course, is Mary's role as the Mother of God, for she is the cause of God becoming knowable and representable to us. Once again it is the Incarnation which is stressed, with the emphasis upon Mary's role in it. The adult-looking Child, who frequently holds a rolled-up scroll in his left hand, is represented like that in order to convey the timelessness of the Son of God; also that he is the Word of God as well as God's Image.

The guidelines laid down by the Council stressed that only the second person of the Holy Trinity was representable. The Father and the Holy Spirit were never directly to be painted. However, in the seventeenth century, at a very low time in the history of icons in Russia, pictures representing the Trinity were imported into Russia from the West. These popular devotional pictures showed the Father as an old man on a throne, the Son as hanging on the cross and the Spirit as a hovering dove. The Great Council of Moscow met in 1667 to remind its Church members of the regulations governing the painting of icons and especially of the Father or the Holy Spirit and strictly forbade any effort to do so.

The Icon we are considering is called 'The Hospitality of Abraham' and represents an historical event. The figures are clearly shown to be angels, as the text of Genesis says they are. What our meditations in Faith help us to understand lies beyond what our eyes tell us; a window or gateway is opened for us on to the Divine.

Chapter Two

Hospitality at Mamre's Oak

Most afternoons, when I get home from work, one of my daughters is missing. She has gone to tea with a friend and her place has been taken by a school friend of one of the remaining children. Although we never use the word 'hospitality' that is what the children are learning. However, it doesn't always go smoothly! Sometimes it is necessary to point out to a daughter that having a friend for a meal, or stay the night, requires a personal effort and perhaps some sacrifice. For example, I might have to point out that you cannot abandon a friend to play on her own, while you go off to watch TV; or, if you are playing at dressing up, you must be prepared to allow your guest to be the princess and let her wear your best dressing up clothes.

Rublev's icon is first and last, as we shall see, about hospitality which entails personal effort, in Faith, and sacrifice of self. The Icon painter interprets the text from Genesis, chapter 18, verses 1-15, on two levels. First the event itself, when Abraham entertains three travellers. Then, well aware that the Scripture text changes from plural to singular and the early Christian writers saw this as a foreshadowing of the later revelation in the New Testament of the Trinity, Rublev captures the Tri-unity of the Divinity in a dynamic and breathtaking way. While both levels entail hospitality, in this chapter we are concentrating on the event itself.

One day Abraham was just settling down to his midday siesta when three men appear before his tent. Instantly and generously he offers them hospitality. At first Abraham accepts what his eyes tell him, namely that there are three men to be entertained, but later he realises that it is the Lord who is visiting him. In typical Eastern fashion, still traditional in the Arab world, Abraham is lavish, 'let me fetch a little bread,' he says, but actually goes off to arrange the preparation of 'a fine and tender calf'. It is important to note that all this occurred, from Abraham's point of view, at the most inconvenient time of the day. We are told that it was 'the hottest part of the day' and Abraham, who was an old man (chapter 17 informs us that he was ninety-nine) would have been settling down for his siesta. His spontaneous hospitality offered to three total strangers therefore demanded considerable personal self-sacrifice. However, Abraham's generosity with both his time and his possessions, the gift of himself in other words, reaps a rich reward.

Earlier, in chapter 15 of Genesis, we read of the promise the Lord made to Abraham, 'Look up to heaven and count the stars if you can. Such will be your descendants' he told him. Abram (his name is changed to Abraham when, in chapter 17, the covenant is made between Abram and God) put his faith in the Lord. Now the angels tell Abraham that in the coming year Sarah, his wife, will bear him a son. This message, in its

20

way, is as important as that brought by Gabriel to Mary: because of his trust in the Lord, Abraham is to have a son, from whom will come Jacob (renamed Israel, Gen 32:28) and the Chosen People. And from within that People, through Mary, will come Jesus and the New People of God. One wonders whether Rublev himself sees this event, under the Oak of Mamre, as being the moment when the gradual build up to the revelation of the mystery of the Incarnation begins: This event when the Lord, we read, appears as a man to Abraham.

Let us, for a moment, consider the figures as angels. The word 'angel' in the Bible means a messenger sent or used by God. In Luke chapter 7 the word is used of human messengers that come to Jesus from John the Baptist, but usually they are spiritual beings (Heb 1:14). The Bible tells us little of what they looked like and there is certainly no fixed form. The halos and wings of the Icon, which conform to our expectations of angel attire, have no basis in Scripture as a reading of the story in Genesis will confirm. So why does the Icon painter use these badges of recognition? Probably simply for that very reason, so that the figures conform to the expectations of the Age. The wings would emphasise the spiritual nature of Abraham's guests and the halos their dignity. The halo was of pagan origin and avoided by early Christian art, but by the end of the 4th century the figure of Christ was accorded one and by the end of the 5th century it was customary to show angels with them. It was not until the 6th century that they were used in pictures of the saints. Abraham saw no wings and no halos, only 'Three men'. It is interesting to consider that if angels can appear to be ordinary men, can, in everyday life, ordinary men and women be messengers used by God?

Some years ago, just before Solidarity burst upon the Polish scene, I went to Poland to research for the book, *Through the Year with Pope John II*. I was very short of material and became convinced that I would find what I needed in Cracow. My family and friends thought I was quite mad, because I knew not one word of Polish, nor anyone living there and I had no definite plans as to where I would find the material or even where I would stay while there. However, I was certain that I had to go and I had received a vague promise of help from the Sons of Divine Providence, who had a House near Cracow.

On my arrival at the Cracow airport, which is really a military airstrip, after the once a week flight from London Gatwick, I had some aggravating problems with Customs. Eventually they released me and there followed an unsettled week when I continually imagined that I was being watched. Everything else went incredibly well. I received some wonderful help from the Sons of Divine Providence, which resulted in a room at the seminary, a mountain of material and the services of an English-speaking seminarist.

At the end of my June week, after Sunday Mass, I left the seminary at 11.00 a.m. to catch a taxi to the airport. I had been advised that this was the only way to get there but I would have plenty of time to arrive by 12.00 for the 1.00 p.m.

22

flight to Gatwick. It was a lovely morning and only five minutes walk to the taxi rank which was beautifully situated under the walls of the Wawel Castle.

There were five Polish people in the queue; after ten minutes and no sign of a taxi, the first two left. By 11.30 a.m. there was only a short elderly lady and myself, and still no sign of a taxi! I was beginning to get very anxious and I had begun to pray very hard. Five minutes passed and the elderly woman, after expressing her mind on the matter in a flood of Polish (I did not need to understand the words, her manner said it all), left me alone. I was left to worry and pray even harder. The minutes ticked by and although I assured myself that all would be well, and I kept reminding God that I really did place all my trust in him, I still worried that this was the only plane for a week to England; that I only had enough money left for the taxi fare; that it was totally impossible to communicate with my wife and reassure her if I did not arrive home that day etc., etc.

God, I decided, helps those who help themselves, so some positive action was called for. As fast as I could, I returned to the seminary, seeking help. I rang the door bell... and rang the door bell! And only then remembered that my English speaking friend had told me that everyone would be out from midday, and it was almost that now. Panic gripped me. I told myself to calm down and think. I searched my luggage for the local guide book and located another taxi rank on the map of Cracow. One was shown across the huge market square, past the Mediaeval Cloth hall. Again I ran and walked as fast as I could to the Square and across it. I kept thinking, 'it's now 12.00 p.m. and I'm supposed to be at the airport.'

Arriving at the opposite corner of the square, near St Mary's Church, I searched for the taxi rank, and could find no sign of one. Then, in desperation, I did a very English thing; I walked across to two grey-clad policemen and asked for help. They knew no English, ignored the airline ticket I offered to show them and dismissed me with a suspicious stare and a belligerent gesture, as their left hands lay across their automatic weapons.

Despair then swept me. Although I was still praying, I felt all was lost, there was no hope now of getting home. Dejectedly I wandered along the pavement to the next corner, where a group of four or five men were standing in a circle talking. In desperation I interrupted them, waving my airline ticket before their startled eyes. They shrugged their shoulders uncomprehendingly and I turned hopelessly away. As I did a voice said, 'Can I help you?' It was the most welcome English I have ever heard. There beside me on the pavement stood a young fair haired woman in her early twenties. She had a companion with her, a girl in her teens. With tremendous relief, and almost disbelief, I explained the problem. 'Come this way', she calmly said. I followed obediently down a street, across some tram lines and then a major road and found myself outside the Lot Airline office. 'They will help you', my guide said. I thanked her profusely and hurried into the empty office. A serious woman in the uniform of the airline appeared and listened to my story: 'You must get a taxi, there is no other way', she told me. She indicated that one was to be found around the corner. It was 12.15 p.m. I left the office feeling washed-out. Fortunately the fair-haired young woman and her friend were waiting outside and together we went to find the taxi-rank. We found ourselves in a treelined square, or rather a long rectangle, with a one-way traffic system. Sure enough there was a taxi rank, but six men were patiently waiting at it!

We were informed by the last man in the queue that there had been no sign of a taxi for over half an hour. This is useless, I thought, after trying hard I'm back where I was an hour ago. 'I'll leave you now', the young woman said. I thanked her, but I must have looked as dejected as I felt, because although she walked away, in a few minutes she was back. As she arrived at my side an airline coach came into the square, and drove up to the back of the Lot Airline office. With raised hopes we ran to where the coach pulled up and my nameless companion went into the bus to speak to the driver. She returned shaking her head saying, 'he's not returning to the airport for three hours'.

Back at the taxi rank I noticed that it was almost 12.30 p.m. Just then a private car entered the far end of the square and parked about 100 yards away. Without hesitation the young woman ran down the road to speak to the driver, presumably to ask him if he would take me to catch the plane. It was a negative reply. I could tell by her manner as she returned. Just at that moment, as she got back to the rank, a taxi turned into the far corner of the square and approached us. The six men in front of me became alert and the young woman took me by the left arm and led me to the front of the queue. She positioned herself between the men and the approaching taxi, with me on her right and she started, I presume, to tell the others why they should let me have the taxi. As it stopped she opened the door, still talking to the men (one of whom was arguing with her), and paused only long enough to say to me, 'Get in'. I stumbled into the taxi; she slammed the door and, as it drove off I could see her, through the rear window, still arguing with the men.

We arrived at the airport with six minutes to spare. I poured all my Zloties, well over the asked-for fare, into the hand of the grateful cabbie. But he was not as grateful as I was!

Relaxed at last, on the flight to Gatwick, I thanked God and thought about all the help I had received. I never knew her name; she had appeared as though from nowhere and I had not even had the opportunity to thank her. When I had been at my lowest ebb and humanly-speaking it had all looked hopeless, then had my prayers been answered. It gradually dawned on me that I had met an angel. Not of course the spiritual kind of being but a human used by God; an ordinary person just like me, prompted by God to give assistance, to act as his messenger. The right person in the right place at the right time, capable of and willing to give assistance.

That was an experience that I am never likely to forget and the memory of it has helped me in a number of ways. First, that if we pray with real faith and trust in God, he will move mountains to help us, even if it is not in the way we expect. Second, angels (God's messengers) are not remote distant figures, we can be angels to one another in life. The help I received on that occasion has already inspired me to be more keen and willing to help others in tiny but important ways. Finally, it has helped me to interpret and understand better some of the angel stories recorded in the Scriptures.

Hospitality comes in two kinds. That which is planned and that which is not. The planned sort, for example inviting someone round for coffee or a meal, is important in sharing and building up relationships. It is also of value because it involves us in unselfish effort. We tidy-up, run the hoover round, perhaps make a cake; then look out for our guest(s) and welcome them with a smile and do all we can to put them at their ease and feel welcomed. In a word, we provide a service, or we minister to them. Hospitality is a form of ministry.

The second kind of hospitality is much more demanding. Viewed from the angle of spiritual development, the unexpected, unplanned and often unwelcome opportunity to offer hospitality challenges us to really put self second. There are few things more irritating than to be happily engaged in something you want to get on with, when an unexpected visitor calls. The natural, and very strong, inclination is to get rid of them as soon as possible, to return to what you want to do. (The same thing applies to receiving a telephone call right in the middle of your favourite TV programme.) Our Faith tells us that we are called to a life of unselfishness, that by dying we live. Hospitality, of which Abraham is our model, takes us to the very heart of the spiritual life, for it is the doing of good, not when it suits us, when it is convenient to exhibit our unselfishness, but when it is asked of us. The person who calls, or rings, may be desperately lonely, depressed or looking for help. To 'get rid of them' as soon as we can is to miss an opportunity of serving Christ.

In our modern society, very sadly, it is hazardous and ill-advised to invite total strangers into your home, particularly if you live alone. But we must not use this as an excuse to dodge our calling. My Polish 'angel' offered me hospitality, in a wide sense of the word, out in the open street. Each of us superficially knows many people who live next door, across the street etc. Every Sunday we gather with fellow Christians, most of whom we hardly know, or know not at all. Far too many nodding acquaintances are in reality 'strangers' to us.

Abraham was richly rewarded for his generosity and we know for sure that we can share the same reward, for did not the Christ say, 'when I was a stranger you made me welcome...for when you welcomed the least person you welcomed me' (Mt 25:35. 40)

Meditation: Before the Icon

1. Under the oak of Mamre, Abraham hurries to entertain the three travellers. It is the hottest part of the day and Abraham would have just settled down for his daily siesta. The visitors could not have arrived at a more inconvenient time. Such unselfish generosity on Abraham's part runs contrary to natural inclination and speaks of many years of unselfish effort, in order to have acquired such a facility. How many times in the past, one wonders, had he shown such kindness to passing strangers? But Abraham had instinctively known it was the right thing to do and now, in his old age, a life time of generosity is about to be rewarded, for the stranger, on this occasion, is the Lord himself.

Let us dwell upon this and the words of the Final Judgement scene recorded by Matthew (Mt 25:35) 'The Son of Man...escorted by all the angels', will say, 'Come, for when I was a stranger you made me welcome.'

2. 'Let me fetch a little bread', Abraham says and then proceeds to provide a lavish meal. Why are we so often mingy with our hospitality, offering as little as we can get away with. Not only in terms of food and drink, but, more importantly, with the gift of our time.

We are each called, from time to time, to be 'angels' to others. They have no doubt prayed for help and God uses the most convenient messenger to hand, me. Yet, so often, we fall short by being mingy with our time and effort when presented with the privilege of helping others.

Let us think of the words in Hebrews 13:1: 'Remember always to welcome strangers, for by doing this, some people have entertained angels without knowing it.'

Chapter Three

The Icon and the Iconographer

We live in the age of the visual. An age when people peer at little screens for both business and pleasure. Never before in the history of our planet has there been so many visual stimuli. The Business world, the Leisure Industry and Educators all know instinctively, if not in detail, what research has shown, namely that we learn 83% of our information through sight, 11% through hearing and 6% through the other senses.

It is against this background that, in the past twenty years, icons have come more and more to the attention of the ordinary Western churchgoer. It seems providential that, at the historical moment when society is increasingly dependent upon the visual, the value of icons has become more widely accepted and understood. In the main they have arrived in Europe and North America through and from the Russian Church.

Christianity in Russia is a thousand years old. It was conveyed there by Greek visitors from Byzantium, who took their icons with them. It was not long after the establishment of the Russian Church that, following the rules laid down in Byzantium, original Russian icons were appearing. The first recorded icon-painter was St Alipy of the 11th century who is regarded as the Father of Russian iconography. Sadly the Tartar invasion of the 13th century destroyed most of the early Russian icons, but by that time a distinctive Russian style had developed. The icons of Byzantium tended to be solemn and stern with a sense of the ascetic about them while, in contrast, Russian icons conveyed a sense of warmth, joy and tranquil peace.

The golden age of Russian iconography was the 14th-15th centuries and this period was dominated by the work of St Andrew Rublev and his friend and teacher St Daniel. As the celebrated film *Andrei Rublev* (1966) directed by Andrei Tarhovsky, showed he was also an imaginative and forward-looking inventor. (The film opens with Rublev experimenting with a hot-air balloon!) His fame however, rests upon his art which left an immense impression upon the 15th century Russian Church. St Andrew, as he is known and honoured by the Russian Church, was a man of exceptional spiritual vision with which was combined an outstanding artistic talent. His work, at the height of the classical period of Russian iconography, is noted for its serenity and joy which is blended with a wonderful depth of spiritual insight. And nowhere is this more apparent than in the Icon we are considering.

Trinity Sunday is an important milestone in the Church's Year, but the Russian Church does not celebrate a separate liturgical festival. The Holy Trinity is honoured with the coming of the Holy Spirit at Pentecost. The events of Pentecost Day are understood as completing the revelation of the Holy Trinity with the coming of the Spirit.

So the Holy Spirit and the Trinity are honoured in two separate parts of the same celebration.

The Old Testament Jewish festival of Pentecost celebrated the giving of the Law on Mount Sinai and acted as a Thanksgiving for the first-fruits of the new harvest. It is also called the Feast of Weeks, being celebrated at the end of the seventh week after Passover. The Christian festival celebrates the coming of the Holy Spirit, the Spirit of love; the gift which concludes and completes the New Covenant made by Jesus, the new Moses, with the Church, the new Israel. With the gift of the Comforter (Jn 15:26), the revelation of the Holy Trinity is complete, so, for the Orthodox Church, this is the time to celebrate the feast of the Holy Trinity. One of the icons especially venerated on this day is 'The Hospitality of Abraham'.

The original Icon, measuring 44 x 55½ inches, is kept, today, in the Tretiakov Gallery, Moscow. It was painted at the monastery of the Holy Trinity and St Sergius, in honour of St Sergius, probably between 1408 and 1410. The theme of the Icon is not original, in fact it is quite common and very ancient in origin. Eusebius of Caesaria (ca. 260-340) in his book *Demonstration of the Gospel* mentions the existence, in his time, of an image of the three visitors to Abraham. All the icon painters, previous to Rublev, depict the historical event more fully, including Abraham, Sarah and their servant with the three visitors. Some of these images place the three angels on the same level as one another in order to stress their equality. St Andrew, in his Icon, concentrates all our attention on the three visitors, excluding Abraham and Sarah, and retains only sufficient of the historical aspect to remind us of its setting. He is the first iconographer to use the structure of a circle in his design. This and his novel and exciting use of colour makes the Icon quite unique and deeply spiritual.

The best way to appreciate the circular structure of the Icon is to move back from the representation before you, take off a ring, (or use something similar) hold it up to your eye and view the Icon through it, so that the ring just encompasses the three figures. You will discover how breath-takingly circular the arrangement is and that the centre of the circle comes where the two fingers of the central figure lay on the table. (We will consider the structure more deeply in the following chapters.)

In the Eastern Christian Tradition, Iconography is as much a language as everyday speech, but the visual form, the line and colour, can be 'heard' in only one way; by remaining still and prayerfully silent before the image. The detailed descriptions we are indulging in here, along with the very individual thoughts and meditations which have occurred to the writer are merely offered to help the reader to get started. Whatever their worth the observations and meditations remain individual; there is certainly no single or 'correct' way of 'hearing' the language of this or any image. Because an icon is a window or gateway to the Divine there can be no limit to what it has to say to those who remain in stillness and silence before it.

Meditation: Before the Icon

1. A wedding ring, or a ring of Religious commitment, is the perfect 'tool' with which to view the circular structure of the Icon, for such a ring reminds us of consecrated love. An unbroken band of precious metal, without beginning or end, is the perfect symbol of such a love.

While no one can even begin to approach an understanding of the Holy Trinity without Faith, it is love which is the gateway to any understanding at all of this great mystery. But love is a mystery in itself! John tells us in his Gospel, that 'God is Love' and 'he who dwells in love dwells in God and God in him.'

2. Whatever we concentrate on in the image, the underlying structure is that of the circle. The Icon speaks to us of Hospitality, of Faith, of Christ as the Way and so on, but underlying them all is love. I may have all the knowledge there is about this Icon but if it is without a loving regard, it will profit me nothing. (1 Cor 13).

3. The revelation of the mystery of the Trinity, Rublev is saying through his Icon, is not an arid truth to be grappled with mathematically, or with triangles and shamrocks, but to be lived in love. Just as we do not wait for a clear definition of love (which is not possible) before giving and receiving love, so too we rob our spiritual life of meaning if we wait upon a better (never to be obtained) understanding of the Trinity before sharing, as fully as we are able, in that circle of love.

Chapter Four

Inviting the Spirit

If you have ever spent a sunny holiday in a dry climate like North Africa, Spain or Majorca you will have noticed, as your plane comes in low to land at London Heathrow or Gatwick, how vibrant and fresh this green and pleasant land of ours appears. I have been struck, on several occasions, by the greenness of our countryside, something I have just taken for granted. It is, of course, one of the effects of living on an island where the rainfall is so plentiful. When we Northern Europeans read scripture passages like 'let the wilderness and the dry-lands exult, let the wastelands rejoice and bloom' (Isaiah 35:1) we are inclined to forget, or perhaps not realise, that in Israel it rains only at two periods of the year.

The figure of the Holy Spirit, represented on the right of the Icon is dressed in blue and green: the blue above the green. Those colours would seem to stand for water and vegetation. Without water nothing can live, neither in the animal kingdom nor in plant life. Blue and green are the perfect colours to remind us of the action of the Life-giving Spirit. The figure's robes speak of the cause and the effect of the new life.

Rublev, in designing the Icon, uses the human tendency to look towards the right first. It is an accepted principle in newspaper and book design that the right page, or right-hand-side of a page or picture is the strongest. The human glance falling naturally first to the right-hand side. You can test this for yourself by picking up any daily tabloid newspaper; you will discover that most full-page advertisements come on the left and the most eye-catching items are placed on the right, pride of place going to the first turn of the page from the front, namely page 3! The same goes for book design. Title pages are always on the right, odd numbered pages, and, when possible, new chapter headings will start on the right and so on. This inclination of the human eye is used to dramatic effect in the Icon, for the 'movement' of the Icon begins on the right-hand side with the figure dressed in the 'new life' colours of blue and green. What more suitable colours to represent Baptism and the work of the Holy Spirit?

As your eye runs up the figure from foot to head you are led on, by the curvature of the body, the bowed head and the direction of the eyes, to the next figure that commands the centre of the Icon. We are not intended to stop on the right-hand side. Hardly have we taken in the colour of the clothes than we are directed on, almost impelled to move our eyes on round the circle. It becomes almost a physical effort to stay with the first figure. This impresses upon us that the Holy Spirit's role is to involve us, then move us on, not to stay with himself. It is clear that we cannot derive full benefit from this Icon unless we begin with the right-hand figure. We cannot journey round the circle of love and become caught up in the very life of the Trinity unless we start the circle's dynamic 'movement' with the Holy Spirit. Which is to say if we do not have Faith we cannot enter the gateway to the Trinity.

Some years ago, a priest who was engaged in pastoral work in South-East London, told me of the following experience which, he said, was as valuable to him as to the young mother involved. It was a miserable grey October day and he had been out visiting for two hours in the afternoon. It had been many years since the parishioners had been visited and the address list was hopelessly out of date. At every door the young priest learnt that parishioners had moved, died or were just not in. At 4.30 p.m. with a depressing sense of failure, he decided to try just one more call before heading back to the presbytery.

A stout middle-aged woman answered the door and told the priest that the Ryans had been gone some time, however, she thought the young Scottish girl who lived in the front ground floor flat was a Catholic. She knocked on the door to her right, and when there was no answer said, 'Must be out with the baby'. He thanked her and went to unchain his bike, parked against the front wall, doing so he almost collided with a pram turning into the garden path. An observant voice from the front door called out, 'Mary, this gentleman was looking for you'. The curate introduced himself to the fair-haired woman, who could not have been more than 18, and she said, 'Come in'.

Mary parked the pram in the hallway, scooped up a tiny baby on to her left arm and with her right hand unlocked the door and again invited the priest to come in. He followed her into the flat, or rather bedsitter, and into the most indescribable mess! The double bed was unmade and littered with dirty clothing. The two tatty armchairs had greasy plates of half-finished food standing on their arms; newspapers and magazines covered the floor around them. A child's dirty nappy lay on the papers beside the nearest chair. The room smelt. The door to a miniscule kitchenette stood open and in full view was an ancient gas cooker with its door open and a small pile of clothes lay in front of it. 'Sit down', Mary said to the apprehensive young priest, proceeding, with her free right hand to move the clothes from the bed to the floor. The curate tactfully chose to move to the nearest armchair, avoiding the dirty nappy, and lifted newspapers and two grimy plates to the floor, and sat down. Mary, who was only a few feet away, sitting on the edge of the bed, unwrapped the baby and held him up to be admired. The priest told me that he tried not to let his surprise register on his face, when he saw that the child had black hair and Chinese features! Although the baby had not yet been christened, Mary told the priest that he was called Robert. 'I'm really glad you've come' said Mary, 'I've been walking around for hours praying for help'. Then she poured out a horror story, as she cuddled her tiny Robert.

About two hours before the young curate called she had been so desperate that she had laid down on the floor in front of the open cooker, with a pile of clothes under her head, and had just been about to reach up and turn the gas taps on, when the baby had woken up and cried. She had instinctively got up to attend to the baby, realised the enormity of what she had been about to do and in desperation had flung her coat on and gone out to walk and walk and, eventually, she said, pray.

Mary told in her distinctive Glaswegian accent, how she had left school, had a terrible row with her family and come to London about fifteen months before looking for work. She had been lucky in finding kitchen work in a large Chinese Restaurant. A relationship had developed with one of the Hong Kong waiters and they had shared the bed-sitter. They had the baby, she said, but were not married. Her parents had not heard from her since she left home and they did not know where she was or the direction her life had taken. Mary admitted that she missed them a lot, especially, she told the priest, her twin brother, Robert. She got regular news of the family, secretly, through an old school friend. That morning she had received a letter, (she reached for a letter lying on the bed pillow, and handed it to her visitor, who glanced briefly at it as she continued her story). Her friend told her that a week before her twin brother had been involved in a car crash and was very ill in hospital. His right leg had been amputated. It was this news which had thrown Mary into a state of total despair, because she desperately wanted to go home to be with her twin, but she felt it was impossible because she believed that her devout Catholic Mum and Dad would not understand about the baby and the Chinese waiter.

After the long story the concerned young

priest asked a few questions and learnt that her young man did want to marry her and was prepared to travel with her to Glasgow, if she could return. The priest, who told me that he had felt totally helpless throughout the story, then suggested the idea that he might ring her parents' parish priest in Glasgow. Mary thought that that might be a good idea because Fr Kelly knew her family very well. My friend left her in a hopeful frame of mind. She told him, as she accompanied him to the door, 'I'd better tidy up a bit' and the priest assured her that something could be sorted out.

That evening my priest friend rang Fr Kelly and told him the whole story. He was relieved to hear that Mary was safe and well. He had known her since primary school and knew how delighted her parents would be to have news of her. He felt he could put the news of the baby and the prospective husband across with no problem. He rang back, as arranged, the next evening, and the parents' joy at hearing his news had infected him and as he told my friend about his visit to them he too felt a warm glow of delight as well. Mary's parents had been told everything and wanted nothing more than to have her, the baby and her boyfriend home with them in Glasgow. And the brother was out of intensive care.

My curate friend couldn't wait to tell Mary the good news and cycled round immediately. He found the bedsitter tidied up, the baby still in her arms and Mary so happy at the news that she burst into tears, leaving the priest feeling rather foolish. She wouldn't stop thanking him, and he said, 'Really, I haven't done anything, I only made a phone call'. A few days later, on their way to the local station, all three called at the priests' house to thank the young curate again, unfortunately he was out visiting, but was pleased to receive their message and he told me he has since wondered how their story continued.

The crucial point, I realised later, in Mary's desperate story was the moment when she said, 'Come in'. Out in the street she could so easily have ignored the priest, or denied being a Catholic or told him to come back at another time. But she invited him in, and that invitation was the vital moment when her life took a turn for the better. The mess in her room was as nothing compared with the mess, she felt, her life was in. That mess was sorted out as a result of the invitation.

The Holy Spirit figure in the Icon invites us into the circle and reminds us that 'Come' is the essential prayer to direct to the Holy Spirit. Mary must have had faith in the priest to have invited him into her home and to have unburden herself to him. We need to invite the Holy Spirit to come to dwell in us so that we can be directed to the Father through the Son and become caught up in the life of the Trinity.

It is no coincidence that the two great hymns to the Holy Spirit, written in the Middle Ages, both begin with the word *Veni*, (*Veni Creator Spiritus* and *Veni Sancte Spiritus*) and the traditional Catholic prayer to the Holy Spirit starts, 'Come Holy Ghost, Creator, Come…'. When the Holy Spirit comes to us, at our invitation, then we are drawn into the family circle of the Trinity. First the Holy Spirit must come and move over the darkness and the mess (Gen 1:2) which, to a greater or lesser extent is within us all. Left alone we can do nothing, only the Creator Spirit can bring order out of chaos. As in the story about Mary, it may not take much, or very long, to sort us out, but it is not something we can do alone, there must first be the invitation.

It is impossible to move to the next figure in the circle and acknowledge who it is unless one has welcomed the Holy Spirit within. 'No one,' Paul tells us (1Cor 12:3), 'can say "Jesus is Lord" unless he is under the influence of the Holy Spirit.' Perhaps in a more conventional and familiar way we might say, 'No one can say that Jesus is the Son of God unless he or she has faith.' Which is exactly the same thing. We have traditionally been more reserved, or more staid in our terms, speaking of 'having the gift of Faith'. But being able to believe is, a sign of the presence of the Holy Spirit.

> 'We can know that we are living in him
> and he is living in us
> because he lets us share his Spirit.'
>
> (1Jn 4:13)

> 'If anyone acknowledges that Jesus is
>   the Son of God,
> God lives in him, and he in God.' (v. 15)

Primarily one does not pray *to* the Holy Spirit, but *for* the Holy Spirit, with the invitation, 'Come, Holy Spirit'. Even the movement within us, the grace to ask the Spirit to 'Come', springs from the action of God himself, so that we can never claim credit for putting ourselves on the road to union with God, but we are still free to say 'Come' or not.

In the totally confusing days following the crucifixion of Jesus, his friends and followers first suffered from shock, for his brutal death had come all unexpected to them; and then bewilderment as the tomb was found empty and their dead friend, Jesus, appeared alive among them. No group of people could ever have been so traumatised, moving from a state of shock and fear to bewilderment and mystification. They retained their former misunderstandings, even asking, as Jesus marked his final appearance to them with the event we call the Ascension, 'Lord, has the time come? Are you going to restore the kingdom to Israel'? Those questions revealed that, even after all that had happened, still they did not understand, still they expected a political solution to Israel's problems. Even after the resurrection of Jesus, the Apostles still expected him to be a military Messiah. Jesus does not allow any disappointment to show as he says 'you will receive power when the Holy Spirit comes' (Acts 1:8). The Apostles needed the Spirit to come and sort out their mess, their misunderstanding. In the fifty days between the shock and bewilderment of the death and resurrection and the coming of the Spirit to enlighten their minds, they did what all good Jews would do and what Jesus had suggested they ought to do (on the Emmaus road the two disciples demonstrate their misunderstanding to the stranger that joins them, 'our own hope had been that he would be the one to set Israel free' (Lk 24:21). Then the Risen Jesus explains 'the passages throughout the Scriptures that were about himself' (v. 27).

The Book of Isaiah seems to have been their principal source of strength, comfort and enlightenment. In chapter 35 they would have found,

> 'Strengthen all weary hands,
> steady all trembling knees
> and say to all faint hearts,
> 'Courage. Do not be afraid.' (vv. 3&4)

Those words would have spoken to their situation. Did they, briefly but very humanly, harbour thoughts of revenge, for what had been done to Jesus? But they would read 'Look, your God is coming, vengeance is coming, the retribution of God; he is coming to save you.' When they read on they recalled the wonderful works of Jesus,

> 'Then the eyes of the blind shall be opened,
> the ears of the deaf unsealed,
> then the lame shall leap like deer
> and the tongues of the dumb sing for joy...'(vv. 5&6)

With their own eyes they had seen the lame walk, the deaf hear. Their friend, Jesus, whom they had presumed would be a political power figure, for that was the common expectation among the Jewish people of the time, had been the opposite to all they had expected. Reading on they found,

> 'for water gushes in the desert,
> streams in the wasteland,
> the scorched earth becomes a lake,
> the parched land springs of water.' (v. 7)

That immediately reminded them of the baptism of John, still practised in places by his followers (Acts 19:4), and the turning away from sin that it signified. Then there was the final command of Jesus, to spread his message about the Kingdom and baptise in water, which signified New Life in the name of the Father, the Son and the Holy Spirit. The water which transforms and gives new life to the dry-lands so that they bring forth flowers and bloom (v. 1) and place one upon the sacred way to union with God. So meditating upon verse eight they came to a new understanding,

> 'through it [the wastelands transformed by
>   water] will
> run a highway undefiled
> which shall be called the Sacred Way:
> the unclean may not travel by it,
> nor fools stray along it.' (v. 8)

It is not surprising that for the next twenty years or more these followers of Jesus called themselves the People of the Way (Acts 9:2) until the name, Christian, is first given to them at Antioch in Syria (Acts 11:26) and eventually replaces it. The exuding joy and happiness of Pentecost Day ('joy and gladness will go with

47

them', Is 35:10) is mistaken at the time, by the crowd, as intoxication. Peter opens the first ever Christian sermon with the arresting thought that the wonderful joy evident in the behaviour of the followers of Jesus does not come out of a bottle, for it is too early yet for the pubs to be open!

The first figure in the Icon's circle directs to the Way. When Thomas asks, 'How can we know the way?' (Jn 14:6), Jesus tells him, 'I am the Way... No one can come to the Father except through me.' So the clear role of the Spirit is to come and set us on the way to the Father.

Occasionally one of my children has announced, as she has come through the school gates at the end of the day, hand in hand with a classmate, 'I've asked Hannah (or whoever) to tea'. 'Hold on,' she is told, 'have you spoken first to Hannah's mummy to see if it's convenient. You must ask first you know.' Even for a child to come to tea some arrangements have to be made; for example, how is she to get home, how long can she stop, etc. There is only one guest for whom no previous arrangements have to be made, and that is the Holy Spirit. The inner mess of the host-person can be unspeakable — all that is required is a sincere, 'Come'. And, as on the day of Creation, the Spirit will move over the chaos and order and life will appear.

The green and blue chosen by Rublev in painting his Icon is full of meaning and the inclination of the figure gives us much to meditate upon as it directs our attention to the next figure.

Meditation: Before the Icon

1. How does the Holy Spirit figure in my prayer life? Do I appreciate that there is only need for the one word, 'Come'? Could this invitation be part of my morning prayer, so that the day's activities and direction is towards the Father.

2. Am I conscious of a 'mess' within me, a disorder that needs the Spirit to move over it? Despite a respectable exterior presented to the World, can I humbly acknowledge my need to pray daily, 'Come Holy Spirit to work a new creation in me and direct me to the Way'?

Chapter Five

Christ the Image and the Way

When Pope John Paul II visited Britain in 1982, with thousands of others I followed his progress with great interest on the television with the mounting regret that I had not been able to be actually present at any of the open-air Masses. At that time I learnt a new song 'Our God reigns' which, as a result of its constant use during the Pope's visit has taken its place in the popular repertoire of many of our churches and congregations; and is especially a firm favourite with the young people.

Every Christian knows that Jesus preached the Kingdom of God, its coming and its very beginning in his own life and teaching. However too few Christians appreciate the meaning of this Good News about the Kingdom. A full understanding is not humanly possible so rich and deep is Jesus' teaching, but anything which furthers our understanding a little is to be welcomed. The 'Hospitality of Abraham' is such an aid, it being a rich source of meditation on the 'Kingdom'. The Icon's second figure to which we are directed by the 'motion' of the circle, speaks to us of this.

Before we pursue that let us examine what we can see. The second angel dominates the centre of the Icon, his voluminous, well-defined robes giving him a prominence and importance not claimed by the other figures. He has about him a strength and solidity that demands attention. This is in keeping with his clothes for under his blue royal cloak there is a tunic with a gold band running over and down the figure's right shoulder, a tunic which is suggestive of the Imperial attire of the Roman Empire.

We are completely free, by the rules of Iconography, to identify this figure as Christ the Lord and his prominence and attire seem to suggest that Rublev wants us to think of him as a regal figure. Christ's appearance may surprise us at first because we expect to see the Lord Jesus portrayed with shoulder-length hair and a beard, but Rublev does not follow the traditional manner of representing Christ. That is deliberately intended because here we are meditating on the Trinity and what is to be emphasised is the unity of love between the three separate persons. To achieve this and to give the representation a timeless quality the faces and hair of all three figures are styled in the same way. The ever-youthful faces of all three suggest that they exist outside time and are not influenced by the changing fashions of history.

The wrist of Christ rests on the table and the first and second fingers of his right hand are displayed to view; you cannot escape noticing it and that is what we are intended to do. Earlier we spoke of the perfect circle which encloses the three figures and the idea of unity that this suggests. The interesting thing is that the two fingers laid on the table are as close as one can get to the very centre of the circle. It has been suggested that the icon painter is referring, by the two fingers, to the two natures of Christ, the divine and the human. So we are back, once again, to a consideration of the role of the Incarnation. Is St Andrew saying that, the centre of this circle of love, that we theologically refer to as the Holy Trinity, is the Incarnation of Christ? It is true that without the Incarnation there would be no human knowledge of the three persons in one Divine nature. Our knowledge of that loving circle only comes from the centre of it.

The figure of Christ the King dominates the Icon and his two fingers are at the centre of the circle. Those two fingers may refer also to the two roles of the Messiah, that of Priest and King. Kingship is only one of the two roles to be played by the Messiah. The Anointed One, will be abused on the cross as a mock king while he is offering himself as a sacrifice to the Father. While the clothes and dominant position of the figure speak of the Kingship of Christ, the two fingers lying on the table, pointing towards the chalice, direct our thoughts towards Christ as Priest. (We will return to the Priesthood of Christ).

'It's alright for him, Sir, he was God'. 'No', I replied as countless R.E. teachers must have done before me, 'It does not help to think of it like that. And it is wrong any way. Jesus was totally and completely a man; manly in every way'. Sniggers from the back of the class and the question from the same region, '*Every* way, Sir?' Ignoring the innuendo, I reply, 'There was only one difference: St Paul tells us that he couldn't deliberately hurt God, his Father. He couldn't sin'.

'Think about this', I continued, 'did Jesus, at the age of 13³/4, just like Adrian Mole, worry about spots on his nose?' That really was a question that caused discussion with the fourth year class! They had been so carefully taught that Jesus is God, Jesus is God... that comments like 'God died on the cross' ran uncritically off their tongues. Christ's divinity had become so all embracing that the human nature of Jesus was given only a nodding acceptance as part of a pat answer when looked for. It carried no real weight or importance.

That particular fourth year class, very typical of most others, had nine years of Catholic Education behind them and not one of them had any appreciation of the significance of the Incarnation or an understanding of Christ as Mediator.

Just in passing, it seems to me, after teaching for some years in Catholic Education that the Docetist heresy of the third century is alive and well and residing in most of our Catholic Secondary Schools and by extension, in most of our congregations. A real appreciation of the true humanness of Jesus is missing because, still, despite a revolution in R.E., too many teachers are fearful lest the children grew up not knowing that Jesus is God.

When I first went to teach in South East London, I learnt that within the boundaries of the parish where I lived, a short walk from the parish church, was a huge G.L.C. (as it was then) Reception Centre for down and outs. It had a capacity of 800 beds; and provided little else, the men having to be out and about during the day. It's proximity to the church guaranteed a regular stream of visitors to the kitchen door!

The parish repository, with the usual assortment of statues and rosary beads, was situated in the run-down hall next to the church. The following story appeared in the parish magazine at the time and was written by Fr Paul Frost, the young assistant priest in the parish. 'One morning I was quite alone sweeping the hall floor when I noticed in the display case (an old glass-panelled bookcase) some small wooden crosses, measuring about 5" x 3" lying on the bottom shelf. "Now that's something I've never done," I thought to myself, "I've never carried a crucifix in my pocket." It suddenly felt so important that I put the broom down and went across the house for the cupboard key and some money. I felt impelled to get one *now*. When my chore in the hall was completed I placed the crucifix in my inside coat pocket and thought no more about it. About three hours later, just after lunch, a call came through from the Reception Centre asking if a priest could come immediately as one of the gentlemen of the road, known to them as "Paddy", was very seriously ill. Equipped with the Holy Oils I went as quickly as I could to the Centre. I had never been inside before and I was struck by the stark, white-washed, simplicity of the place. There was no one much about, except for the warden (or supervisor), who took me through a large hall into a side room where there were four beds. Lying on the first one, just inside the door on the right-hand side, was the sad figure of Paddy. He lay on his back, covered by a single blanket, his face was ashen and his eyes were closed. "He's not long with us," remarked the warden, adding, as he turned to leave, "the ambulance is on its way." There was no bed-side locker, no chair to sit on and no sign of any possessions. I knelt on the floor, close to his head, and bending close to his ear asked if he could hear me. There was no response, so I took hold of the rough-skinned hand that lay along the top of the blanket and said, "If you can hear me squeeze my hand." I was pleased and relieved when there was a very definite tightening and loosening of the hand in reply. "It's the priest, Paddy", I said, "Would you like me to anoint you with the holy oils? Squeeze my hands if you want to". There was another squeeze. After the anointing and the prayers spoken into his ear, the warden appeared in the doorway with the word, "the ambulance is here". I desperately wanted to do something more, then I remembered the crucifix in my pocket. I held it to Paddy's lips and told him what it was. The hand tightened and loosed. I told him I was giving it to him as a little present to take to hospital with him. The hand squeezed and seemed momentarily longer than before. I pressed the crucifix to his lips again and told him it would be in his left hand, the one that I had been holding. He understood. The ambulance men were hovering behind me. I laid his left hand, holding the crucifix across his chest. As they lifted him off the bed I was suddenly struck by the utter desolation of the scene. Paddy had nothing and no one. It was Calvary all over again. He was going naked out of the world with nothing but the crucifix in his hand.

As I walked meditatively back to the presbytery I felt quite upset and immediately rang a neighbouring parish to speak to the curate who was the hospital chaplain. Fortunately I just caught him as he was leaving to visit the hospital. He said he would look out for Paddy. Later that evening he rang back to tell me that Paddy had died in the ambulance on the way to the hospital.' (*Contact Magazine*)

It had been such a thought-provoking experience for the priest concerned. He told me it made him realise how wonderfully God works. He had never carried a crucifix before and as far as I know he has never felt the need to since. Paddy had left the world grasping his only possession, he had nothing but Jesus, and him crucified. And what more was necessary? To have only Jesus was to have everything. The Kingship of Christ asks us to be stripped of the world and to have nothing that is more important to us than Jesus. The great St Bernard of Clairvaux's favourite saying was 'To prefer nothing to the love of Jesus' (Lk 14:26).

The Icon's central figure of Christ as *Imperator*, dominant as it first appears, is a little disconcerting. If you cover the head of this figure and then look at the Icon you will find yourself expecting the figure of Christ to be looking ahead, straight at you, as indeed he does in other Icons.

57

His body is full-forward, but when you uncover the head you find that, surprisingly, he is directing his gaze to the figure on the left. The inclination of his head and the glance of the eyes to the circle's third figure moves us and our praise and adoration on.

A glance. What do we read into a glance? All day long we convey messages through body language and eye contact. As we know so well a brief glance can convey a message of love or hate; sympathy or disdain and so on. The glance of the Christ figure is one of concentrated love. You cannot look into the eyes of the Son of God and not be compelled to look where his loving gaze is directed, the Father. Christ is not a king that holds our love and loyalty to himself, he hands it on to the Father. Christ, the King, is our Mediator, our way to the Father.

This reminds us of the beginning of the concept of kingship among the Chosen People and the dependence that the early Jewish kings had upon God. They realised and acknowledged that the Lord God ruled his People through them. In the Book of Samuel we read how, when the prophet Samuel was old, the elders of the People visited him and asked to have a king, like the nations that surrounded them. Samuel was not pleased at what he interpreted as a rejection of God ruling his People.

> 'Obey the voice of the people,' God said, 'give them a king. It is not you they have rejected; they have rejected me from ruling over them'. (1Sam 8:7)

So Samuel went to Saul to anoint him as king (1Sam 10:1) saying, 'the Lord has appointed you prince of his heritage'. 'Prince', for the Lord was still intending to rule his People and the early Jewish kings understood that they were God's viceroys appointed by him and leading the People in his name.

With the passing of time this understanding was lost. It was to be more clearly re-established, forever, in the Kingship of Christ. To have 'only Jesus' is to acknowledge complete dependence and allegiance. Dependence on Christ and allegiance to him draws us into union with the Father.

'That's the third time I've called you for your dinner'. 'Turn round and stop talking. I won't tell you again!' Whether at home with the children or at school in the class room I find myself saying much the same things. There is absolutely no doubt that obedience is the most difficult of virtues for a human to acquire. It is no wonder that the very first sin recorded in the Bible, from which all the Human Race's ills, it is believed, have flowed, is the sin of disobedience. Disorder springs from disobedience. There can be no loving atmosphere in a family-community where there is no obedience; there can be no advance in knowledge in a classroom where obedience is not expected and given.

So only obedience to God could bring order and unity to the Human Race and only through obedience to God could love and knowledge grow once more. St Paul tells us that Christ, the Second Adam, gave God a perfect obedience, even unto death (Phil 2:8). That obedience is expressed for us in Rublev's Icon in the loving glance of the second figure.

Jesus was the most perfect human being, not because he did not wear glasses or use a hearing aid, but because he gave to the Father the obedience which required a union of wills. However, this obedience was not automatic, it sprang from a human being and as we have seen, humans have difficulty in bending their wills to another. A reading of Mark 14:32-42 (the earliest written account of the agony of Jesus in the Garden of Olives) makes it quite clear that Jesus did not want to suffer. He pleaded in prayer to be saved. In his prayer Jesus reminds God that He is all powerful and can do anything, even save him from the impending arrest and suffering. After much pleading and a struggle with himself Jesus says, 'But let it be as you, not I, would have it.' Obedience is given but only after a very human struggle. Thirty-three years or so before, his mother had been asked to do God's will and she had said to God's messenger, 'let what you have said be done to me.' Obedience is the key.

The words of the Lord's Prayer remind us, every time we say it, that the Kingdom will come only by doing the Father's will ('thy Kingdom come, thy will be done'). Jesus exemplifies those words for us perfectly. He is *the* Man (which is the meaning of the title he liked to use, 'the Son of Man') in whom the Kingdom of God had come. All that we have said above is summed up for us by Rublev in the glance which the Christ figure gives to the third 'angel'.

Obedience can be given out of fear or out of love. The first motive can result in an obedience that is given reluctantly in opposition to the real wishes of the person concerned. Such an obedience is imperfect and not the kind that God seeks from us. 'If you *love* me,' Jesus says, 'you will do what I ask' (Jn 15:10). So true obedience is an expression of our love. As all the saints of the past have shown by their lives there is no more perfect way to show love of God than by seeking His will and doing it. In fact there is no other way to union with God than by the way of obedience; and an obedience motivated by love. When we read of Christ's complete obedience to God, 'even unto death', we are speaking of his measureless love for the Father. All this can be seen, by the eye of Faith, represented in the Icon by the glance.

So, in summary, in the Icon the first 'angel' speaks to us of faith and the second of love, expressed in obedience. As there is a symbol of faith above the head of the first figure, so there is a symbol of love above the head of Christ. The 'tree' in the historical scene, portrayed by the Icon, is the oak of Mamre, but it can also remind us of other important trees in Scripture. Pre-eminently there is the tree of knowledge of good and evil (Gen 2:17). This, of course, is where Mankind's sad story of disobedience began. Jesus spoke of the fruit of the tree, 'by their fruits you shall know them (Mt 7:20) and, as we have seen, obedience is the fruit of our love of God. There is too the tree of the cross, the sign of Christ's total love and obedience. So the tree above Christ's head can be interpreted as the symbol of love.

Meditation: Before the Icon

1. To have *only* Jesus. If we dwell upon that thought it becomes frightening. We like to surround ourselves with all sorts of 'necessary' material things. Why are we so attached to them when we know very well that we will leave the world the same way that Paddy did, naked and facing death alone. We will have 'only Jesus' with us then, if we have developed a relationship with him *now*.

2. Paddy could not have sunk, socially, any lower, yet at the moment that really mattered he had the last sacraments, a priest by his side and the symbol of the love of Jesus in his hands. Does our social standing really matter very much? Does it matter what others think of us, as long as Christ is our King and we are seeking his will in our lives?

3. Jesus of Nazareth did not automatically do what God asked. There was a tremendous internal battle which is emphasised for us in Luke's Gospel where he says 'he prayed even more earnestly, and his sweat fell to the ground like great drops of blood' (Lk 22:44). A servant, Jesus said, is not greater than his master, so we can expect to have times when the struggle within, to find or do God's will, will be a bitterly fought one. Do we shy away from such a struggle, give in and take the easy way out? We cannot say 'Yes' to God without first saying 'No' to ourselves.

Chapter Six

The Mysterious Accepting Father

As the introduction to this book mentions the words you are reading at this moment were put on paper against the noisy background of a vibrant family with four children, all under 12 years of age! Some of the writing has taken place in the early morning before they are about or late in the evening (not a favourite time); sometimes at snatched moments at a weekend, with the constant threat of interruption. One such recent disturbance was the urgent and familiar call from my wife, 'Speak to them, will you, they are not coming when I call them'. Assuming my most authoritarian school-master voice, I went to the foot of the stairs and commanded, 'Come down here, straightaway, NOW'. A stampede of four small figures came running.

Even in these liberated days the phrase, 'Wait until your father gets home' is still heard and in many families the father is still the final port of call when there is a question of authority and discipline.

There is a certain air of receptive expectancy about the third 'angel' in our Icon. The same expectancy that is associated with the father in the parable Jesus told of the Lost or Prodigal Son.

'While he was still a long way off, his father saw him and was moved with pity. He ran to the boy, clasped him in his arms and kissed him tenderly'. (Lk 15:20)

This father is not cast in the role of a disciplinarian, or an authority figure, but of an anxious Dad who waits and longs for his son to come home of his own free will. When he sees him coming he cannot wait but runs to meet him.

A priest, whom I have known for many years, told me the following true story and allowed me to write it up as it appears here.

'It was many years ago, but I still remember it clearly. It happened one long June evening, Tuesday, I think. The day had finished earlier than usual at about 7.30 p.m. and for a change there were no parish meetings or clubs to visit. Although there were letters on my desk waiting for an answer and plenty of papers to be sorted through, I suddenly felt at a loose-end and gazed idly out of the window of my bedsit into the quiet London street in which the Presbytery was situated. I noticed a stocky man of average height, wearing spectacles, pass by on the pavement opposite. I'm sure I wouldn't have noticed him had he not glanced up in my direction as he passed. The net-curtaining shrouded me from his gaze. Perhaps, I thought idly, he's casing the joint! (Not such an idle thought in that part of London). My daydreaming was disturbed and I was puzzled when he passed by again two minutes later, in the opposite direction. Again he glanced across the street. Had he noticed something wrong outside, I wondered, a drainpipe hanging loose, or should I phone the police and report a suspicious character. Would he pass again? Sure enough, two or three minutes later he came again into view. I went downstairs to the front door to observe events from behind the net curtain over the glass panel in the door. A long period elapsed, three or four minutes, and I had just begun to doubt whether he would re-appear, when there he was walking slowly passed. While I had been waiting I had resolved to go out and speak to him, if he passed again, so I opened the door and crossed the street. "Excuse me, can I help you, only you seem interested in our house". A real look of relief crossed the man's face. "Could I speak to you," he said. "I've been trying to pluck up courage and ring the bell."'

'We had a coffee and talked for nearly two hours. It was the beginning of a friendship that has lasted to this day. I can still remember well the way he opened our chat. "I didn't think you and the Church would accept me. I'm not a Catholic, my wife hasn't been to church for years; we're not married in the church — everything's in a bit of a mess!" After a few months the marriage was 'put right', their two sons were baptised and just over a year later Ted himself was received into the Church. A very down-to-earth London docker, he became the very best of Catholics, involved in parish work, particularly with the young people, with whom he had a great rapport. Due to Ted's influence his sister-in-law, who had rejected the Church for many years was anointed in hospital just before she died.

'Ted's boys joined the youth club and through them Ted became involved in the management of the club. The "Grove" was popular and success-ful and ran smoothly without any real problems; but one evening the Eagle gang arrived at the door. They were led by a skinny malevolent looking character called "Boo". The other black-jacketed gang members were also only known by their nicknames. I was called to the door when they attempted to enter. They tried to prove they were all Catholics (none of them were) by recit-ing the Hail Mary and I was just trying to explain that they could not come in when Ted arrived on the scene. He took me to one side and said,"You must let them in". "No fear," I replied, "We want no bother". "You must accept them", Ted said. "It's a church club". We argued for a minute or two, but Ted was insistent. "You must accept them". "Alright", I said, "But you are respon-sible for them". He went out to speak to them, while regular club members asked me what was going on.

'It worked, not easily or without a few minor problems, but it worked. Not many weeks later Ted asked if the club could be open on a Sunday evening, as well as the Friday. "Yes," I said "after the 6.30 p.m. Mass, as long as you are there to keep an eye on things." "No problem", replied Ted, and from then on he gave up his Sunday evenings so that the Eagles particularly had somewhere to go on a desolate Sunday evening.

'Then one Sunday, Ted did something I would never have dreamt of doing. He invited the Eagles to the Sunday evening Mass and they came. Ted and the black leathered group in heavy boots and metal chains occupied one of the back pews. In an over-enthusiastic moment, one Sunday, Ted asked three of the slouching group to help him take up the offertory collection. I shall never forget the faces of several elderly devout Catholics as these figures stomped upto the front of the church, did some strange sort of bob up and down and turned to face the congregation to take the collection!'

The priest who told me the above story said that Ted's work among the young did untold good; the Eagles remained club members and out of trouble with the police. I believe they have long been settled as respectable citizens. Through his first encounter with the Church Ted learnt that when the Father accepts us we too must be accepting of others. What else does our prayer to the Father, 'forgive us our trespasses as we forgive those who trespass against us', mean if it does not mean that the Father's acceptance of us is the model of our acceptance of others. The Father used the priest to accept Ted, which led to the acceptance of his family; and the Father used Ted to accept the young people. (Quite obviously God the Father had seen that he could not entrust the acceptance of the young people to the priest, as events proved!)

Our eyes have taken us 'round' the Icon from the first angelic figure. What we now see is the slightest of the figures which has an air of mys-

67

tery projected by the ethereal, 'translucent' clothes. Rublev has brilliantly succeeded in conveying the mysteriousness and unknowable quality of the 'Father'. Blue, the only colour common to all of the 'angels' is clearly there under the shimmering translucent outer garment. Are we being reminded again of the importance of Baptism? Are we to recall how the believer only comes to participation in the life of the Trinity through Baptism?

Even as our eyes are directed by the other two figures to the expectant face of the Father, we are compelled by the angle of the body to move down first to the hands and then on to the feet. Then the circle is complete; our eyes have returned almost to where they began. It is interesting to note that the Father alone holds his staff with both hands, distinct from the other two. Perhaps it is being suggested that the Father is the source of all authority and power. In his life Jesus speaks of his authority and power as coming from the Father.

> 'All authority in heaven and earth has been given to me.' (Mt 28:18) and that statement is followed by the command,
> 'Go... baptise them in the name of the Father and of the Son and of the Holy Spirit.' (Mt 28:19)

We have already noticed that above the head of each of the angels is a symbol. There is, rather indistinctly, a mountain above the 'Spirit', there is a tree above the Son and, solid and clear, above the Father is a house. Not a structure that has much to do with reality, but that is the style in icons. It is representative, on the historical event level of meaning, of Abraham's dwelling, outside of which the hospitality of the Patriarch takes place. However, in the deeper spiritual meaning of the icon it may refer to that text from John, 'In my Father's house there are many rooms' (Jn 14:2). It is of interest to note that this sentence comes just a few verses before the words of Jesus where he describes himself as the Way (v. 6). This is, in turn, followed by Philip's request, 'Lord, let us see the Father!' Then follows the beautiful exposition by Jesus of his union with the Father and the promise of the gift of the Spirit. It is surely no coincidence that all these relevant texts come side by side. It seems likely that Rublev had them all in mind when he was painting the Icon.

No interpretation can be or need be definitive so it is possible that the painter was also drawing our attention to Isaiah 56:6-7.

> 'Foreigners who have attached themselves to Yahweh to serve him and to love his name… these I will bring to my holy mountain. I will make them joyful in my house of prayer. Their holocausts and their sacrifices will be accepted on my altar, for my house will be called a house of prayer for all the peoples.'

The Icon was painted for liturgical use and the 'house' is there above the 'Father's' head and the holy mountain at the top right. The group sits around the 'altar' table. The Icon was intended

69

for use in a house of prayer and each one of us, that stands meditatively before it, is called to be a temple of the Holy Spirit or a 'house of prayer'.

To enter prayerfully into the dynamic circular motion of this Icon catches us up into the Father's house of prayer, or family of prayer. We invite the Spirit to 'Come' and in that Spirit we offer ourselves and all we are and do to the Father through Christ the Way. The Father accepts, for he cannot refuse anything or anyone offered to Him in union with the obedience and love of his Son; and the circular life or action starts all over again.

Whatever interpretation we adopt or discover for ourselves the sheer richness and depth of meaning will remain. However, the second interpretation does not seem to take due note of the prominence and vital importance of the second figure. The text from John does that, but Rublev could well have had several texts in mind; for what Scripture text can embrace the fullness of the Trinity?

As our eyes arrive at the bottom of the Icon we become aware, for the first time, of the heavy black outlining of the feet of the 'angels' on either side. These feet have brought the visitors to Abraham's tent, where they are invited to rest. Are we intended to think of the 'angels' as pilgrims? Certainly the staves they carry remind us of pilgrims and the pilgrimage of life.

The prodigal son's pilgrimage (Lk 15) took him away from his father's house but he chose to return humbly seeking a servant's place. The

70

generous expectant father would only have him back as a son.

Ted's pilgrimage brought him and his family back to the Father; he would be the first to acknowledge that since then he has had to seek the Father's loving acceptance many times. His confident faith assures him that in his Father's house there are many rooms and the Father will always accept him and his love offered in union with the Son.

Meditation: Before the Icon

1. What image does the word 'Father' conjure up for us? That of a disciplinarian, an authority figure, or a loving Dad? Has our relationship with our own father influenced our thoughts about the fatherhood of God?

2. To be accepted and loved just as we are, warts and all, that is what the Father is always offering. All we need to do is find our Way to him; Christ will direct our love and obedience. All our prayers should flow like Christ's to him.

3. The Father is mysteriously distant but the loving glance of the Son draws us to him. We are drawn to an understanding of his ever-present willingness to accept us whatever we have done on our pilgrimage. We cannot travel without needing rest and the Father will always be there to give us that.

Chapter Seven

The Place at Table — the Priesthood of Believers

In our family Thomas is only two but he is the greatest upholder of orthodoxy! When meal times arrive he insists in sitting in *his* place; when Grace is said before the meal he joins his hands neatly in front of him and then looks round to check that everyone is doing the same thing properly. Sometimes thoughtlessly, but often deliberately, one or other of his three older sisters has clasped her hands or laid them in her lap. Thomas protests loudly and points at the offender! Only when the whole family is conforming to Thomas' standards of rectitude can we get on with the prayer.

When Nanny and Grandad come for Sunday dinner there is another seating problem. All four children want to sit next to Nanny (poor Grandad doesn't get the same treatment!), and there is a squabble about who sat next to her last time. Interestingly, from a grown-up point of view, sitting opposite Nanny will not do; it has to be on either side of her! These are the positions of favour and anywhere else is of no consequence.

It is no different in the classroom. There is a great deal of upset if friends cannot sit together. Being with friends and loved ones is very important to us all.

Reading between the lines of John the Evangelist's account of the Last Supper there appears to have been a little jockeying for positions round the table on that occasion. This would relate to the little incident when James and John's mother arrives and asks Jesus (probably to the embarrassment of the twins) if he will keep the best places next to him for her sons.

At the family celebration of Passover the Jews have the quaint traditional practice of leaving an empty place at table, along with a glass of wine, for the Prophet Elijah, just in case he comes again, during the meal. The story is told of the little Jewish boy who, throughout the Passover meal kept looking at the empty chair and finally, towards the end of the meal, piped up with, 'It doesn't look as though Elijah's coming, can I have his wine?'

In 'The Hospitality of Abraham' there is an empty place at table. Not for Elijah but for the Icon viewer, whose eyes have 'journeyed' round the circle of love. In the life of a family, unity is never more visibly evident than when the family sits down to eat together. There is a sense in which the 'family' circle portrayed in the Icon is not complete. There is a vacant space in the foreground, left (deliberately) by the painter. A space that is crying out to be filled. The more one sits meditatively before the Icon the more one feels compelled to occupy that empty place at table.

We believe that Baptism makes each of us an adopted child of God, adopted into the very life of the Trinity. Nowhere is this belief given more concrete expression than in Rublev's Icon. Baptism gives me a place at the table. Only by meditating before the Icon can we begin to appreciate the great dignity to which we are called. 'Praying' the image we become caught up into the very life of the Trinity.

We have already thought deeply about the circular construction of the Icon and the circle of Love that is the life of the Trinity (as far as we can humanly approach the mystery). In stark contrast to this flowing 'motion' in the circle there is a strange rectangle in the foreground, set into the front of the table. It is angular and disturbingly out of tune with everything else in the Icon. Its prominence demands attention and once it is noticed it seems to distract from the 'life' of the image. What is it? What does it mean or stand for?

Let us consider a number of observations. First, the box-like rectangle is too prominent and central to be insignificant to the meaning of the Icon. It is situated, in one of the places in an altar where the martyrs relics are traditionally deposited. A custom dating from the time when the Eucharist was celebrated in the catacombs. There on the top of a tomb of one of those who had died witnessing to Christ with their lives the 'Breaking of Bread' was celebrated. Are we intended to remember the martyrs and how they gave their lives for Christ?

Second, we should note that some have thought that the rectangular opening represents the world. The four corners standing for the four corners of the world (we have to recall that the

Iconographer would have believed, as people of his time did, that the earth was flat and had four corners). So the aperture could represent all the nations of the world, north, south, east and west.

If we put together all that we have noted above, we might be led to think of all those from every corner of the world who have preached the Good News and witnessed with their lives for Christ. The text from St Matthew's Gospel comes to mind, 'Go make disciples of all the nations; baptise them in the name of the Father and of the Son and of the Holy Spirit' (28:18).

The 'world' of course can have another meaning in Scripture. It can also mean 'worldly', opposed to things of the Spirit. This understanding would relate well to the way in which the rectangle seems to clash with the general motion and feel of the Icon. It certainly does distract the viewer from the circular dynamic 'action' of the image, and this is rather like the conflict all Christians experience in their lives.

There is no correct answer to the meaning of the rectangle. What is interesting is that if, in meditation, the viewer does 'step' into the place at table, taking his/her baptismal place, then the angular box is obscured and disappears from view! Those who are baptised, in the name of the Trinity, renounce the world when they make their baptismal promises. 'Do you renounce Satan...? the candidate for Baptism is asked and only after the firm, 'I do', does the Baptism proceed. To occupy the place at table is to say 'no' to the world. However, to live in the world the life of the committed Christian is to be a witness to Christ. For some Christians to dare to be different from the worldly values about them will lead to suffering, so perhaps all our thoughts about the strange rectangle come together. Rublev seems to be saying to us, through his Icon, 'step into your place as a child of God, opposite the Son of God; put worldliness away and live the life of the circle of love.'

Due to the work of the Second Vatican Council we understand better now the unity of the three sacraments of Baptism, Confirmation and Eucharist. These are once again, after hundreds of years, thought of as 'the Sacraments of Initiation'.

While Baptism incorporates the believer into the life of the Trinity and membership of the community of believers, the anointing of Confirmation strengthens the believer to witness for Christ and the Eucharist sustains the life of the Spirit within the Christian. In our Icon all the Sacraments of Initiation are represented. In order to take one's place, by Baptism, at the table of the Eucharist, one obscures the place where the relics of the witnesses for Christ were traditionally placed. In other words one takes the place of the witnesses of the past to be a living witness nourished by the sacred food from the table around which the Trinity's love circles.

My youth, spent for the most part at a Catholic Boarding School, was dominated by a cheery but distant figure. Corbie, or more formally Monsignor Ernest Corbishley, is remembered in the Southwark Archdiocese for being the first Rector of St Joseph's College, Mark Cross, Sussex. I remember him for, among other things, his boring spiritual talks. They were not boring because of the content but because of their repetition. He always had the same thing to say. ' "He who is faithful in that which is least", he would say, "is faithful in that which is greater" (Lk 16:10). Boys, life is made up of little things, lots and lots of little things that you do and say. And they are all important. Use your Morning offering; offer all the little things to God. That is the way to holiness.'

Corbie, who died in 1959, would be pleased to know that his repetitious message had a lasting effect upon at least one of his pupils. I have, over the years, learnt to appreciate more and more the truth that he hammered home and quite obviously lived by.

Christ, the Letter to the Hebrews explains in great detail, is our High Priest who 'has offered one single sacrifice for sins... he has achieved the eternal perfection of all whom he is sanctifying' (10:12. 14). In spite of the way we speak and act, there are not many priests, men set aside to work in our parishes and churches, but one in whose name they function. From Christ the High Priest they receive the appellation, 'priest'. Our High Priest makes use of them, for we know that when our local parish priest stands at the altar he does not say, 'This is the Body of Jesus', but, 'This is *my* Body'.

That is mysterious enough, but we can also read how we are all priests.

> 'Brothers, through the blood of Jesus we
> have the right to enter the sanctuary, by a

new way which he has opened for us, a living opening through the curtain, that is to say, his body. And we have the supreme high priest over all the house of God. So as we go in, let us be sincere in heart and filled with faith, our minds sprinkled and free from any trace of bad conscience and our bodies washed with pure water.' (Heb10:19-22).

With Faith and through Baptism we have the *right* to enter into the presence of God, but only through our supreme High Priest. Is this what we have been meditating upon before the Icon? The Son of God, as priest, offers himself and all his love and obedience to the Father, the perfect sacrifice.

Not an hour in the day passes but we are made aware of our frailty as humans. The complaint that rises to our lips, the glance that should be controlled, the impatient gesture that is going to wound another. Every thinking believer is only too well aware of the imperfections that crowd daily life, yet there is the imperative that comes from Jesus, 'Be perfect just as your heavenly Father is perfect' (Mt 5:48)! Surely, we think to ourselves, it's impossible! In another place Christ Jesus says to us, 'Pray continually' (Lk 18:1) and Paul takes up the same imperative, 'Pray all the time', in his Letter to the Christians at Ephesus (6:18). Not possible, we are forced to conclude, life must go on.

The Apostle Paul seems to have thought long and deeply about those apparently impossible imperatives. And he offers a most wonderful solution. As a former good Pharisee, Paul knew that at the time of the great covenant between God and the chosen people on Mount Sinai, God said 'I will count you a kingdom of priests' (Ex 19:6). Over the following centuries the People of God brought their animal sacrifices to the men who represented them before God, the descendants of Aaron. Our supreme High Priest, Christ the King, by his once-and-for-all gift of himself sweeps away the need for bloody animal offerings and Paul reminds us that our worship is a spiritual one (Rom 1:9) and it is ourselves that we offer, 'our bodies as a holy sacrifice, truly pleasing to God' (Rom 12:1). Peter in his First Letter takes up the same thought,

> 'Set yourselves close to him so that you too, the holy priesthood that offers the spiritual sacrifices which Jesus Christ has made acceptable to God, may be living stones making a spiritual house.' (2:4. 5)

So as Jesus was, on Calvary, both the priest making the offering, and the offering itself; he offered himself. So too we are a royal priesthood, by virtue of our Baptism and, we are the offerings as well; we offer ourselves.

'Nothing is more certain dogmatically', Teilhard de Chardin says, in his inspiring *Le Milieu Divin*, than that human action can be sanctified. "Whatever you do", says St Paul, "do it in the name of our Lord Jesus Christ." And the dearest of Christian traditions has always been to interpret those words to mean: intimate union with our Lord Jesus Christ.'

The representation of the 'three angels' shows a living dynamic relationship and we are reminded that Christ is not a dead once-upon-a-time priest, 'since he is living for ever to intercede for all who come to God through him' (Heb 7:25). Our offering to the Father, in union with Christ's priceless offering, takes place now and every 'now' in the future.

'Pope Elopes'. With this eye-catching headline, journalist Dorothy Parker won a competition in Algonquin, U.S.A., for the most startling imaginative caption. As we are all very well aware, we live in the age of the Sensational, the New and the Different. A company director was telling me quite recently that all he has to do is to have the words NEW LINE stamped across a product in his Company's Mail Order catalogue to receive a deluge of orders for that particular item. 'People want to be different, to be one up on their neighbours', my friend said.

For many people in Western Society today the REAL is the different and the new; the boring and the deadening is the daily work and the life of chores and the daily duties. In fact of course, the latter is all too real and for most people without any meaning and purpose. But for the Christian it should not be, need not be so. '*Whatever* you do,' says St Paul, AND HE MEANS 'whatever' (Col 3:17). The washing up, the house cleaning, the ironing, the shopping and so on, done 'in the name of our Lord Jesus Christ' gives perfect praise and glory to the Father. It is the

81

Priesthood of the Believer in action. It is all so beautifully simple. It is taking our place at the table; having prayed, 'Come, Holy Spirit', and with the deepening of Faith and Love that comes from that prayer, we offer all that we are, have and do to the Father by way of the Son, our Priest and King.

Meditation: Before the Icon

1. Concentrating upon the rectangular cavity in the centre foreground, do I feel a certain conflict with the motion, round the circle, that my eyes want to be caught up in? How important are 'things' to me, my possessions, my work, my career? Does worldliness conflict with the life of the Spirit within me?

2. Does taking my place at the table and trying to realise my great dignity as a child of God feel frightening, awe-inspiring? Does it enrich my life today?

3. Does every day begin with a morning offering? Is this day and everyday going to be a priestly day as I offer myself and all that I will do today to the Father through the Son?

4. Can I find time every day to look back to see how I have humbly witnessed to Christ during the day?

Chapter Eight

'He Who Eats This Bread'

Two years ago a child was killed on a busy road near where we live. The body was taken away, sawdust was swept over the blood, the mess was cleaned up and the traffic flow and the hustle and bustle of life continued as before. There is nothing to mark where a precious young life was suddenly extinguished, but I still cannot pass the spot without seeing in my mind's eye the blue lunch box with its Star Wars motive lying in the middle of the road.

Relatively few people are buried these days; there is almost an unseemly urgent need to tidy the dead body away as conveniently and as quickly as possible and then, except for those intimately involved, pretend that the person never existed.

My grandmother, with whom I lived for a few years as a child (my grandfather having died some years before), was straight out of the traditional Catholic mould. As she got older, refering to future events, she would say, 'you'll be doing... when I'm pushing up the daisies'. At the time I did not understand this quaint way of referring to her own death and what might or might not happen afterwards. However even then I knew that she prayed fervently for a happy and holy death. Her prayer was answered.

For some years before my mother's sudden death, she was in the habit of qualifying plans for the future with 'if we are spared'. Educated in pre-Vatican II devotional practice, like her mother before her, she prayed for a death that would be fortified with the sacraments of her Church. Her prayer too was answered.

Prior to the reforms of the Second Vatican Council there was an exaggerated emphasis, in popular devotions, upon death. Praying for a happy and holy death, gaining indulgences, observing the First Nine Fridays etc. were all seen as essential parts of the devout Catholic's prayer life. The teaching of Pope John XXIII's Council restored to the centre of theology and spirituality an understanding and appreciation of the vitality and joy of the Resurrection of Christ. The emphasis now was to be upon sharing in the life and love of the Risen Christ; one important way to that was clearly shown to be through a better understanding and appreciation of Baptism.

Rublev's Icon is 'modern' in the sense that it is completely in keeping with the teaching of the Second Vatican Council. Frequently we have referred to the role of Baptism and the dignity of the baptised. The Risen Jesus dominates the Icon and the 'image' would not work without his presence presiding in the centre as the Way to the Father.

Looking at the Christ figure flanked by the two 'angels' presiding over the 'eucharist' upon the table, we are reminded of the scene at Emmaus when the Risen Jesus sat down to eat with the two shocked and disillusioned disciples.

They only recognised him when 'he took the bread and said the blessing; then he broke it and gave it to them' (Lk 24:30). We need Christ and the food he offers if the vitality and joy of the Resurrection is to be real in our spiritual lives. More than that it is also the cause and promise of our belief in life after death and our strength in facing realistically the certainty of physical death. For he who 'eats this bread will live for ever' (Jn 6:51).

Christians, of course, are ordinary citizens like everyone else subject to the same pressures and daily tensions. We are all equally in danger of being influenced, often very subtly, by the consumerism which pervades our Western Society. Easily influenced too by the current desire to pretend that death does not happen, or at least does not happen to one's self, to other people possibly but not to oneself and one's immediate family. It is as unhealthy to under emphasise death as to over emphasise it. The old Catholic tradition of praying for a happy and holy death was not unhealthy for it ensured a mature realism which kept everything in proper perspective.

Concentrating on the centre of the Icon we can see that lying between the two fingers of Christ, resting on the table and the rectangular aperture is the symbol of the Eucharist. To the right of it the index finger of the Holy Spirit seems to touch the altar table. This must surely remind us that it is the action and power of the Holy Spirit that makes the sacramental presence of the Incarnate Son of God available to us. This availability is so that we may unite ourselves to the Son's offering of himself to the Father and so that we may be spiritually fed. The food is for our spiritual growth; he or she who does not grow, dies. (It is not the sole way of receiving spiritual nourishment but the one very specially given to us by Christ himself).

Some months ago, my father, still mourning the loss of my mother, was very suddenly and unexpectedly taken ill and rushed to hospital in the middle of the night. I was alerted early the next morning by my sister-in-law, who telephoned to say 'the Hospital registrar has had a look at him and says we must think in terms of two to three days at the most'. Shocked and bewildered I questioned her and she repeated, 'Dad has been given two days to live'. While I drove the ninety miles to the hospital, alone and in a stunned meditative silence, I really 'felt' the importance of life, life in itself. Everything else suddenly became a nonsense. The money worries that had been plaguing me, the anxieties about my work, the decorating jobs that needed doing in the house, everything that had concerned me a few hours before were now as nothing, with no value or importance. Faced with the reality of death, life fell into perspective. Perhaps, I remember pondering, that is where our likeness to God, spoken of in Genesis, resides. When we say we are made in the image and likeness of God we mean, we live and love, as God is existence and is Love. It's simple, I thought, all that matters is how we live and how we love. They are the only two important issues in life. Everything else is so much junk.

(Thanks to prayer and a skilful medical operation my father survived and is today fit and well.)

According to a traditional story, St Francis of Assisi, was hoeing his garden and was asked what he would do if he were suddenly to learn that he was to die at sunset that day. He said, 'I would finish hoeing my garden.'

St Francis had a proper appreciation of the Incarnation; he knew that God is to be found as much in hoeing the garden as by kneeling in a candlelit church. If his hoeing was offered prayerfully and lovingly to God the Father through and in union with the Son, as it surely was, it was the most perfect of prayers and the ideal preparation for Sister Death.

It is not easy for the ordinary human, even for those with Faith and Baptism, to appreciate that God is to be found, loved and served in the small, ordinary daily things of life. Humans naturally tend to think of God in grand terms. After all he is the Almighty, the all-knowing, the Being without beginning or end, so he must surely be conceived in the grandest of terms. But God himself tells us that we should not just think of him as transcending everything.

As the Lord God demonstrated to Elijah when he was hiding from his persecutors in a cave on Mount Horeb; we must not think of God just in great events,

> 'Then Elijah was told, "Go out and stand on the mountain before the Lord." Then the Lord himself went by. There came a mighty wind, so strong it tore the mountains and

shattered the rocks. But the Lord was not in the wind. After the wind came an earthquake. But the Lord was not in the earthquake. After the earthquake came a fire. But the Lord was not in the fire. And after the fire there came the sound of a gentle breeze. And when Elijah heard this, he covered his face with his cloak and went out and stood at the entrance of the cave. Then a voice came to him, which said, "What are you doing here, Elijah?" ' (1Kgs 19:11-13)

The Incarnate Christ is present to us in the Church and in the Word of God, but also as food. How ordinary, plain and simple! If we had been present in the Bethlehem stable we would have seen a normal-looking baby; if we had called into the carpenter's workshop at Nazareth we would have spoken to an ordinary looking man. When we look at the bread and wine on the altar table we see ordinary looking unleavened bread and wine. The wonder of God is how he uses the ordinary.

A question that I have sometimes pondered is did my grandmother and my mother die happy and holy deaths because they prayed regularly for it, according to an earlier devotional practice or did they obtain that grace because neither missed receiving the Eucharist at least once a week. Not a question that can be answered. Perhaps the answer lies in the word 'perseverance' or 'fidelity'. A strength that comes from the sacramental Bread and Wine.

Above we spoke of the revelation to Elijah

that God is to be found in the gentle breeze not in the thunder and earthquake. Just a few verses earlier we read how God fed Elijah for a long journey.

> ' "Get up and eat, or the journey will be too long for you." So he got up and ate and drank, and strengthened by that food he walked for forty days and forty nights.' (1Kgs 19:7)

Would not the pilgrimage of life be too hard and difficult for us if it were not for the strength that we receive from the Eucharist?

Having Faith and being baptised is not enough, we need to be faithful, to have fidelity in our lives. It is no great thing to believe that there are three persons in one God, nor to have been baptised, unknowingly, as a child. What we are called to, as a knowledge and appreciation of our Baptism grows, is to live the life of the Trinity. To faithfully, day by day, in terms of the Icon, journey round the circle of love, again and again and again, etc.

> 'Through fidelity we situate ourselves and maintain ourselves in the hands of God so exactly as to become one with them in action. Through fidelity we open ourselves so intimately and continuously to the wishes and good pleasure of God, that his life penetrates and assimilates ours.'
>
> (Teilhard de Chardin, *Le Milieu Divin*)

Meditation: Before the Icon

1. 'I would finish hoeing my garden'. So said St Francis. If I was told that I had just a few hours to live, would my daily attitude to my work and life be prayerful enough for me to say, 'I will finish my day as I always live it'. Or would I rush off to kneel in the nearest church?

2. If I am offering myself now and every day to God do I think positively and prayerfully about my approaching death as a final offering of all that I am to God?

3. How central to my life is celebrating and receiving the Eucharist? Do the words, 'he who eats this bread will live forever' (Jn 6:51) reassure me about death and the life to come?

4. 'Through fidelity', Teilhard de Chardin says, we open ourselves to the will of God. Life sometimes seems so boring; we feel insignificant with little achieved. But fidelity and perseverance is everything; let us place our complete trust in the God of Elijah, the God of little things.

Chapter Nine

The Guest Within

Our local paper, the *Evening Echo*, very recently carried the story of a tragic incident at the Southend Carnival. A Mr Griffiths, a retired teacher, was on a day trip from Harrow Weald, Middlesex. He was standing at the front of the crowd, in Marine Parade, watching the carnival when suddenly his attention was distracted. A toddler, Danny Brooke, just 20 months old, wandered off the pavement right into the path of a motorcycle skidding out of control. Without a moment's hesitation Mr Griffiths threw himself in front of the boy and took the full impact of the heavy motor cycle. He was rushed to hospital with multiple injuries, but died soon after admission. Danny was treated for shock at the same hospital, but was soon discharged. A Police spokesman said, 'Mr Griffiths saved the child's life'. An eyewitness said, 'It all happened so quickly, it was over in a flash. We did not realise the seriousness of the incident until later.'

Mr Griffiths' heroic, Christ-like, action was not recognised for what it was or appreciated until people had the opportunity to piece the story together and interpret what had occurred.

This book set out to try and interpret the signs and symbols to be seen in the 'Hospitality of Abraham'. Reflection upon these in meditation should lead us to a better (although never complete) understanding of the life of the Holy Trinity and the way in which we can become caught up in that same life; although it is not always easy to recognise the signs or choose between possible interpretations. Further to that an appreciation of its meaning for *me* has got to occur.

Years ago, while I was involved in social work in South London I was summoned to an elderly client's house by a neighbour. The old gentleman's wife had been taken into hospital a few days before and the neighbour had promised to keep an eye on him for her. She had become concerned when his curtains were not drawn by mid-morning and he was not answering the door. As a strong smell of gas was evident from outside the front door, the police had also been summoned. I arrived on my bike as a patrol car drew up outside. The Police Officer shouldered the front door open and we stepped into a dark gas-filled hallway. With a hand over nose and mouth we found our way to the back living-room and kitchen. The policeman went to open the back door while I opened the curtains and raised the sash window. I gasped in the fresh air and turned to see the constable turn off an unlit gas fire. He told me that he had already turned off two rings on the gas cooker. Then we saw the body. In the gloom I first thought I was looking at a pile of clothes on the floor, then I realised it was the crumpled body of Mr Stevens. He had been dead quite a long time. The policeman radioed for the police surgeon and I went next door to a neighbour's and phoned for the local priest.

Then the policeman asked me to help him look for the suicide note. I was stunned and wondered what had compelled this very reserved devout Catholic to take his own life. We could find no note.

The priest came and did what he could and I was still there when the police surgeon arrived. It did not take her long to deduce that Mr Stevens had died of a heart attack and not from being gassed. It was subsequently shown that the onset of the heart attack had affected his sight. He had attempted to light the gas fire but had failed to put the match to it properly; the same thing had happened at the cooker. He had then sat down at the table and almost immediately collapsed on the floor. The clues were all there but the police officer and I had misread them. We had concluded that it was suicide, instead it had been a sudden lonely death in sad circumstances.

According to style Iconography never presents scenes within dwellings. Even the Upper Room event at Pentecost is portrayed in the open. This is not a problem with this Icon, because Abraham's hospitality is offered in the open under the Tree of Mamre. Did Abraham appreciate from the beginning that his visitor(s) were Divine. He does use the singular, in verse 3, when addressing them. 'My Lord, I beg you, if I find favour with you...' Did Abraham then read the signs correctly, or was it later that the realisation dawned; perhaps when the promised son was born. It is impossible to tell.

One thing is certain. The guests were treated with great respect and generosity, but they were kept outside. They were not entertained within Abraham's tent.

About two years ago, before we moved to our present home, my two eldest daughters liked to play with Jacky, a neighbour's daughter. She came to play at our house several times and stayed to tea. When, eventually, Helena and Louise went to her detached house to play, they were only allowed to play in the garden, although they were permitted into the kitchen for tea. They learnt from Jacky and her brother that no child was permitted into the lounge unless accompanied by an adult! Their mother said that they made the place untidy!

Although Abraham must have had a good reason for not entertaining his guests within his tent, hospitality is surely warmer and more complete if offered within one's own home.

The Jews of the time of Jesus travelled hundreds of miles from all over the Roman Empire in order to visit Jerusalem, their Holy City. This was where they believed the Presence of God was located. In the Courtyard of the Priests was the large open air altar where the carcasses of the people's offerings were burnt. The smoke rose up in worship, up, they believed, into the very presence of God.

The sacrifice of Jesus did away with such a crude form of worship. Mark, in his Gospel, recognises that fact when he writes the following in his Passion story.(15:38) 'Jesus gave a loud cry and died. The veil of the Temple was torn in two from top to bottom.' The worship of the temple was finished, the perfect once and for all sacrifice had just been offered.

Judaism had worshipped a remote God; Christians were invited to address God as 'Abba, Father,' and the Incarnate Son of God says,

> 'If anyone loves me he will keep my word,
> and my Father will love him,
> and we shall come to him and make our
>   home with him'. (Jn 14:23)

And again,

> 'You will understand that I am in my
>   Father,
> and you in me and I in you.' (Jn 14:20)

> 'Make your home in me as I make mine in
>   you.' (Jn 15:4)

The Apostle John says,

> 'No one has ever seen God
> but as long as we love one another
> God will live in us
> and his love will be complete in us.
> We can know that we are living in him
> and he is living in us
> because he lets us share his Spirit.'
>
> (1Jn 4:12)

The Apostle Paul writes,

> 'I live now not with my own life but with
> the life of Christ who lives in me.'
>
> (Gal 2:20)

> 'May he give you the power through his
>   Spirit

for your hidden self to grow strong,
so that Christ may live in your hearts
through faith.' (Eph 3: 16)

It is abundantly clear where God can be found according to the New Testament. Whether we think of it as the Indwelling of the Holy Spirit or the presence of Christ in the faithful Christian, it comes to the same thing. The Holy Trinity, Father, Son and Holy Spirit, is found within, for where one person is present, the whole circle of love is. By Faith and Baptism each of us can say, 'I am host to the Guest within, in whose name I was baptised'. We have an even greater privilege than Abraham, we entertain the Three in One *within*. This is the continual and traditional teaching of the mystics of the Church.

'Since the human soul is capable of receiving God alone, nothing less than God can fill it; which explains why lovers of earthly things are never satisfied. The peace known by lovers of Christ comes from their heart being fixed, in longing and in thought, in the love of God; it is a peace that sings and loves and burns and contemplates.'
The Fire of Love (Richard Rolle)

God dwells in our hearts by faith, and Christ by his Spirit, and the

'Spirit by his purities; so that we are cabinets of the mysterious Trinity.'
(Jeremy Taylor)

'Poor creature though I be, I am the hand

and foot of Christ. I move my hand and my hand is wholly Christ's hand, for deity is become inseparately one with me.'

(*St Symeon, the New Theologian*)

In the summer I had to go to see my Bank Manager in Tunbridge Wells. I decided to make a day of it and took along my eldest daughter and a picnic for us both.

The business completed we had a look at the famous Pantiles (Regency shopping arcade) and then drove out into the countryside to find a suitable spot for our picnic.

Afterwards I took my daughter on a nostalgic visit to the village of Mark Cross, where for six years, in the 50's, I had been at St Joseph's College. We viewed the building, now a school of ballet, from a distance and in reminiscent mood I recalled little anecdotes.

There was one place, long and often in my memory, that I particularly wanted to visit. Along the Brickfield Lane I found the place, overgrown, the gate collapsed into the undergrowth, but it was there as I had remembered it, although it was much further from old Rotherfield Station than I had imagined. (It is interesting how our memories often play us tricks about size and distance). This had been the route of one of our organised class walks, in line, wearing our caps and always in the care of one of the prefects!

In my last year, out with a very small group of seniors, I had stopped at the gate to wait for some slow walkers to catch up. Those I was with wandered ahead a little and I was alone. Then it happened, like a bolt out of the blue. It might be termed a spiritual experience but for me it was simply that the penny dropped, as we say. I suddenly appreciated something that had escaped me before. It was all at once vividly real and vitally important. 'I live now, not I, but Christ lives in me' (in the Douai translation I was accustomed to then) means just what it says. Christ really is within me, now. Christ dwells by faith in my heart. It suddenly became clear, my prayers must not drift up, like incense, into the presence of God, a God away up and out there somewhere. Personal prayer is to the One within.

It was a wonderful and very real experience. It left me hungry to read all I could find about the Guest Within (but there seemed to be very little available, the only good book I found was the rather dated *God Within Us* by Raol Plus SJ). I wondered why the College rector, an evidently holy man, had never spoken of so great and important a spiritual truth. Perhaps, I concluded, he had but I had not taken in what he told us because I had not been ready for it. (Just as a child will only walk or read when he is ready for it; spiritually it seems to be the same, the grace of God can only move us on a step when we are ready.)

Our daily actions, the ordinary simple routine things of each day, like St Francis hoeing his garden, can be offered as gifts of love to the Holy Trinity within. In themselves these actions are worthless but, sanctified by the Holy Spirit and offered to the Father in union with the love and obedience of the Son, they become of infinite value. (See again the passages on the Priesthood of Believers).

When we really understand and appreciate this we can, with St Paul, say 'Glory be to him whose power, working in us, can do infinitely more than we can ask or imagine.'

Who could ever imagine such a truth. The circle of love that my eyes see in the Icon actually exists, lives and acts, within me!

Meditation: Before the Icon

1. Have I ever considered the question, where do my prayers go? Do I vaguely imagine them drifting up and out there, or is prayer addressed to the Guest Within?

2. Can I close my eyes and 'see' the Icon. Now can I start to appreciate that the image, the circle of love, is actually, now, within me?

3. A growing awareness of the Guest Within should result in the evidence of peace and joy in our lives. How do I share this gift of peace and joy with others?

1000 YEARS OF FAITH IN RUSSIA

PIMEN, Patriarch of Moscow
interviewd by **Alceste Santini**

In this first interview granted to a Western
journalist, Pimen, the supreme authority
of the Russian Orthodox Church, here
responds to some 55 complex and
disparate questions: peace, human rights,
genetic engineering, abortion, divorce,
sexual freedom, ordination of women,
ecumenism, ecology, and nuclear threat.
The interview throws considerable light
on the many aspects of the life of the
Church in her complex history and in her
very life today as she relates to the State in
a regime of separation of powers. The
authoritative words of the Patriarch,
uttered on the eve of the commemoration
of the millennium of the advent of
Christianity in Russia, acquire the value of
a documentary and as such is an
extraordinary document.

Pages: 212   214x138mm
ISBN 085439 274 2   Price: £7.95

CHURCH, ECUMENISM & POLITICS

New essays in ecclesiology
by **Cardinal Joseph Ratzinger**

The basic issues Cardinal Joseph
Ratzinger addresses to in this collection of
articles and papers are: the question of
the nature of the Church, its structure, the
ecumenical scene, the relationship of the
Church and the world. And "for a first-
hand familiarity with the Cardinal's
present thinking one cannot do better than
turn to this collection... There is in the
Cardinal's theology an intertwining of an
opstimistic view of the human benefits
conferred by the Church with a
pessimistic view of the abandonment of
reason and loss of nerve of much
contemporary thought... For those who
want theological stimulation and
occasional provocations or simply a better
acquaintance with the Cardinal's thought,
this book is to be warmly commended."
(*The Tablet*, 5 March 1988)

Pages: 278   215x138mm
ISBN 085439 267 X   Price: £9.95

MARY FOR TODAY

by Hans-Urs von Balthasar

What does Mary mean for today's men
and women? That is the question Hans-
Urs von Balthasar sets out to answer.
Dogmatism in language, and one-
sidedness in Marian cult have, in many
ways, shifted attention from the fulness
and deepness of Marian mystery. The
distinguished Swis theologian shows here
new possibilities to meet Mary in a more
authentic way. With a masterly
combination of theological consideration
and spiritual meditation, he explores what
the New Testament tells us about the
Mother of God and places Mary on the
horizon of our time, portraying her as icon
- model of convincing praxis of faith:
Mary, mother of believers; Mary, the
Church in origin.

Pages: 72 178x107mm
ISBN 085439 266 1
Price: £2.50

THE HAPPINESS OF GOD
Holiness in Thérèse of Lisieux

by **Susan Leslie**

According to the best masters of
spirituality a solid foundation of holiness
is to give oneself to God in such a way
that *his good pleasure* becomes one's joy.
Therese of Lisieux had this magnificent
obsession: *to see God happy.* As she lay
dying in September 1897, at the age of 24,
she claimed that all her actions had been
performed with that single aim. *Making
God happy* was Thérèse's programme of
life and holiness. This is the target she,
even today, sets before the multitude of
"little souls" whom she hopes to carry
along her "little way" to heaven.

Pages: 96   178x107mm
ISBN 085439 272 6
Price: £2.95

THE STATIONS
OF THE
RESURRECTION

Scripture Devotions for Easter Season

by *Ronald G. Gibbins*

"I am happy to commend this short book, *The Stations of the Resurrection*, for its devotional and scriptural content and as an imaginative way of helping people to meditate on the life of the Risen Christ among us. This should be a book from which all Christians can draw inspiration **D.Worlock, Archbishop of Liverpool.**

This book has various practical uses: by an individual as a private devotion, by a house group or congregation; by ecumenical groups.

Pages 88
ISBN 085439 268 8
Price £2.95